The Moon Race

Written by
Cath Jones

Illustrated by
Dave Williams

Every year, there was a race from the Earth to the Moon and back.

Every year, someone from the Smith family entered the race. This year, it was Mum's turn.

The James family had won last year. Could Mum beat them?

Then, the very next day, Mum fell off a ladder! Now she was out of the race. Who would race in her place?

"What about Pearl?" Nana Smith said to Mum. "I think your daughter would be perfect!"

A week later, Pearl was sitting in the space port. She stared at the line of spaceships on the runway.

Could this be happening? Was she about to enter the Moon Race?

A speaker buzzed. "Are you ready to race?"

Scott James was sitting next to Pearl. He was flying the James spaceship. He whooped and punched the air.

"Let's go!" he yelled.

As they walked to their spaceships, Scott said, "You're very brave, Pearl. You dare to race me. No one beats me!"

He's not going to scare me, Pearl thought. Scott's just a bully!

Pearl sat down in the spaceship and pushed some buttons. The thrusters burst into life.

But just as her spaceship took off, a hatch popped open. Pearl's brother, Ben, had sneaked onto the spaceship!

"I wanted to race to the Moon too," Ben said with a grin.

"It'll take at least three days to reach the Moon," Pearl told him. "And that's just half-way in the race. So you can learn how to fly the spaceship. It will pass the time."

As they got nearer to the Moon, they spotted Scott's spaceship.

"Let's pass him," Ben said.

Then suddenly a wormhole appeared in front of both spaceships!

Scott pushed his spaceship's booster buttons. The force from the boosters pushed Pearl's spaceship into the wormhole.

"Hang on!" yelled Pearl, as their spaceship was sucked into the dark wormhole.

"What's a wormhole?" Ben asked.

"It's like a tunnel," Pearl explained. "But it can take you to any place and to any time. We just don't know where – or **when** – we will come out."

"So where will the wormhole take us?" Ben asked.

"Wormholes are a mystery. No one knows where an exit will be," Pearl said. "Or what point in time it will be."

"What if we never come out?" Ben shrieked. "I can't bear it!"

"Try to stay calm," Pearl told him.

Then, in a moment, they shot out of the wormhole!

"Where are we?" Ben asked.

"I can see Earth!" Pearl yelled. "That wormhole was a shortcut back home!"

A speaker buzzed. "Earth calling Pearl. Welcome back!"

"Your spaceship is the first one back," the voice said. "You are the winner of this year's race!"

Pearl and Ben whooped with joy. Scott had helped them win!

"We met a wormhole on the way," Pearl told them.

"We thought so," said the speaker. "It led you back to Earth. But it led you back in a different **when**. You are seven days early! The Moon Race starts tomorrow!"